NATIONAL PARKS
OF
AMERICA

NATIONAL PARKS
OF
AMERICA

James Murfin

GALLERY BOOKS
An Imprint of W. H. Smith Publishers Inc.
112 Madison Avenue
New York City 10016

This book was devised and produced by
Multimedia Publications (UK) Ltd.

Editor: Marilyn Inglis
Production: Arnon Orbach
Design: Terry Allen
Picture Research: Virginia Landry

First published in the United States of America 1985
by Gallery Books, an imprint of W. H. Smith
Publishers Inc., 112 Madison Avenue, New York,
NY 10016

ISBN 0 8317 6327 2

Typeset by Keene Graphics
Origination by The Clifton Studio Ltd, London
Printed in Italy by New Interlitho SpA, Milan

CONTENTS

THE WIND, THE SAND AND THE SEA

TODAY A LITTLE MORE LAND MAY BELONG TO THE SEA,
TOMORROW A LITTLE LESS. ALWAYS THE EDGE OF THE SEA
REMAINS AN ELUSIVE AND INDEFINABLE BOUNDARY.

RACHEL CARSON, *The Edge of the Sea*

The wild and fragile shores of the United States are ever-changing masses of great stone sculpture and delicate beaches, stretching from the fog-bound coast of Maine, around the Atlantic and Gulf sands and marshes, to the rugged sea cliffs of the Pacific and the glacial bays of Alaska. The secrets they hold, the beauty they reveal, the vast geological time they measure, all shape the thin edge of the North American continent. A thousand environments and ecosystems link a massive chain of life at once so stoically set in time that evolution is imperceptible, and yet so delicately balanced that one footprint can inexorably alter it forever. But for a few windows here and there, where the far-sighted have sought to preserve and protect, the magnificent primeval splendor that once *was* now begins to fade.

Fortunately for all, the United States Congress and the Department of the Interior, through the good sense and splendid management of the National Park Service, along with other conservation agencies, have set aside vital portions of America's coastal lands as preserved and protected areas. None of the urgent legislations came too soon; in fact, some came far too late to repair more than two centuries of devastation. The footprints of time will never be eradicated along some sandy shores; in some cases, however, slow, gentle, methodical care offers promise.

ACADIA NATIONAL PARK

Previous page left *Remnants of ancient headlands, these pinnacles of rock, or seastacks as they are commonly called, stand off the coast of Washington state. These particular seastacks occur at Point of the Arches, Olympic National Park.*

Previous page right *John Muir, the great naturalist, was struck by the starkness of ice and snow and newborn rocks which form Glacier Bay National Park. Ptarmigan Bay, pictured here, is part of the park.*

America's national parks begin at Acadia in Maine where the sun first touches the United States' shores, a place so utterly lonely that the geological clash of elements goes on with enormous force, heedless of life in any form. In this park, perhaps like no other, the evolution of land is seen and felt, for it goes on before the eyes. Yet, a few steps away from the shore, the dark green primeval forest calms the senses and sets all else into another, unknown time. The thundering geysers of ocean spray drift away and the landscape melds into glacial ponds and great stands of spruce, hemlock, fir, and pine. There is a quietness here, a remoteness, stranded in time as the Gulf Stream, flowing nearby from the south, meets the cold Labrador Current from the north, and envelops all in a dense fog.

The white man first came to Acadia in the earliest days of North America's exploration, no doubt using the island now known as Mount Desert, the highest elevation on the eastern seaboard, for navigation. French explorer Samuel de Champlain sailed into Frenchman Bay in 1604; a century later Louis XIV gave the

island to the Sieur de la Mothe Cadillac, who called himself Seigneur des Monts Deserts. But the real settlers of Acadia were farmers and fishermen, antecedents of the legendary, hardy "down-easterners," who now fill the harbors with Maine's great fishing fleets. About the middle of the nineteenth century, they, and the extraordinary beauty of the land, were "discovered" and before long Mount Desert became a summer vacation-land for some of America's best known and wealthiest families — the Fords, the Rockefellers, and others. It was they, and individuals like Charles W. Eliot, president of Harvard University, and George B. Dorr, a wealthy Bostonian, who, seeking land set aside for both private and public enjoyment, began the first national park to be donated to the federal government — some 6000 acres in 1913 — and the first east of the Mississippi. First established as Sieur de Monts National Monument in 1916, it was renamed Lafayette National Park in 1919, and then changed to Acadia National Park ten years later. Constantly growing since, the park boundaries now include more than 38 000 acres on Mount Desert, the Schoodic Peninsula on the mainland, and the spectacular cliffs of Isle au Haut.

Shrouded in mist, the dark, green coniferous forests fringe the rocky shoreline of Acadia National Park.

Above right *Great stands of spruce, hemlock, fir and pine cover the glacier-scoured valleys of Acadia National Park.*

Below right *The remains of granite mountains, carved by glaciers and drowned by invading seas form the rugged coastline of Maine's Acadia National Park.*

Below *The extraordinary beauty of Acadia was "discovered" about the middle of the nineteenth century. Since that time it has been a summer vacation-land.*

What happened at Acadia is geological conjecture: perhaps as much as 375 million years ago, molten rock raised the earth's crust to form the core of what is now called the Mount Desert Range of the State of Maine. Slowly the lava cooled and solidified into pink granite, evidence of which we see today. But then came great glaciers that carved an entirely new landscape, giant blankets of ice two miles thick that cut valleys and sheered mountain tops and hewed out rock walls and steps. Somes Sound, the only fjord on the east coast of the United States, is an example of the tremendous force of the glacial age. The low lands to the east gave way to the weight of the ice and disappeared beneath the sea, thus forming the coast as we know it. Now the seasons, the cold and sun, the rain and rushing tides inexorably dig away at the shores.

In and around this jagged shoreline is one of the East Coast's finest examples of tidal zones. Tidepools, pockets of seawater stranded in rockbound basins, brimming with aquatic life of all kinds, are the primeval confluence of land and water, and here at Acadia they echo twice a day the vast mysteries of man's relationship with the sea. No other coastal park in America demonstrates more vividly, in so small an area, the incessant ebb and flow of this planet's evolution, than does Acadia National Park.

CAPE COD NATIONAL SEASHORE

If Maine is "down east" to the indomitable Boston Yankee, then Cape Cod National Seashore is indeed the "lower cape" of the Massachusetts curved peninsula that juts out and northward so defiantly into the Atlantic breakers. Thoreau put it more dramatically: "Cape Cod is the bared and bended arm of Massachusetts; the shoulder is at Buzzard's Bay; the elbow, or crazy-bone, at Cape Mallebarre; the wrist at Truro; and the sandy fist at Provincetown."

Never mind the direction in which the arm points, one still goes "down" north to Provincetown, nearly due south of Acadia, and no less precious in the chain of preservation. Yet, unlike Acadia's tough, granite cliffs, Cape Cod's fragile environment is vulnerable to both nature and man's abuse. Constantly eroded by the wind and sea, the shifting sands of Cape Cod's arm bear little resemblance to the fertile topsoil and hardwood forests the Pilgrims found when they stopped here briefly in 1620. In their diaries they wrote that the island was "lofty" with trees, so much so, in fact, that some who went ashore got lost in an expanse of forest. "It is compassed about to the very sea with oaks, pines, juniper, sassafras, and other sweet woods," they wrote, and the earth was rich, "like the Downes of Holland." Only in rare, protected areas does there remain even the suggestion of this original landscape — the Massachusetts Audubon Society sanctuary at Wellfleet preserves some ancient trees.

Cape Cod is a land of unmitigated human abuse. For centuries now, since settlers first felled the trees for ships and overgrazed the land for livestock, careless, wanton exploitation has consistently plundered the landscape of its vital vegetation. Soil loosened and was carried away with the winds; sand dunes piled high and buried what was left of shrubs and grasses. In more recent times, paved roads and human trampling of plantlife brought its own form of destruction. Only in 1961, when the United States Congress authorized the Cape Cod National Seashore, did there appear any signs of stopping this shameful loss. Now, within the protected boundaries of the park at least, plantlife is slowly but steadily coming back; stunted pines and oaks dot the hills, shrubs reclaim the moors, and deep-rooted grasses are once more stabilizing the shifting dunes.

Below Cape Cod's fragile environment is vulnerable to both nature and man's abuse, but slowly plantlife is returning.

For many years it was thought that Cape Cod had simply risen from the sea, washed in toward land by tides and currents. It made sense. As the seasons went, the beaches were first built and then torn away, demonstrating quite clearly to all that this was the constant evolution of the ages. All of Cape Cod is, in fact, what geologists call a moraine, a spinal ridge of coarse sand, clay, and loose gravel left by retreating glaciers some 10 000 years ago.

Still the sands shift as they did before inhabitants were faced with the "scientific evidence" of other forces. Irrespective of how Cape Cod was formed, its shape is ever-changing. Islands are formed and then ripped away; harbors are shifted from one storm to another; land is joined and then separated. The British *Somerset*, which ran ashore near Highland Light during the American Revolution, has been buried and resurrected a dozen times in the last two centuries by the changing sands. The Atlantic shore has been slowly buffeted away by the wind and sea; even today, where high bluffs remain at Truro, 130 feet above the water, the relentless erosion steadily whittles the land away at the rate of several feet a year. The 40-mile Outer Beach, the Provincetown Hook to the North, and the narrow sand spits of Nauset Beach and the Monomoy National Wildlife Refuge, were all created at the expense of great cliffs that once reached two miles to the east. Within the last 50 years at Truro alone, the highlands have receded 160 feet, so fierce is the Atlantic's winter surf.

One is aware of these changes at the Marconi Wireless Station site at Wellfleet, where the Cape is only one mile wide. Much of the cliff has eroded away since Guglielmo Marconi first built his towers here in 1901. Another place to sense nature's power is near Provincetown where giant dunes are even now encroaching on the highway.

What will happen to Cape Cod? The National Park Service protects a 40-mile section from Chatham to Provincetown. Perhaps vegetation will take hold and survive; chances are it will here quicker than elsewhere on the Cape. But there will be a constant struggle. Every summer, thousands of vacationers will have their way. When they leave, the Cape will once more begin to revive itself. Meanwhile, the relentless Atlantic waits its turn.

Below *Cape Cod is what geologists call a moraine, a spinal ridge of coarse sand, clay and loose gravel left by retreating glaciers some 10 000 years ago.*

Fire Island National Seashore

Just 20 miles from New York's city limits, on the very edge of the nation's largest population concentration, lies Fire Island National Seashore, the most northern of the preserved Atlantic coastal barriers, a narrow, 32-mile-long island off the south shore of Long Island. It stretches from Democrat Point on the west to Moriches Inlet on the east, facing the Atlantic and protecting the waters of Great South Bay and the mainland of Long Island at its back. People have created 17 separate communities on Fire Island, primarily for summer recreation, but great efforts have been made to preserve the natural life here, whether it be a hidden hardwood grove or long-legged herons stalking stiffly through grassy wetlands. Here, too, wild geese and brant fly over the salt marsh and occasionally a startled deer dashes off through the thicket.

Throughout the year the park presents different faces at different seasons. In winter the beach is deserted and the ocean booms as it assaults the land. The forests are stark as the leafless trees stand bare against their evergreen neighbors and the sky is full of clouds. Springtime brings a greening to the land and a muting of the ocean, while the noise of new life quickens in the marshes. Rafts of migrating waterfowl bob on the protected waters of Great South Bay. Summer is the hot, golden sun on the white sands of the beach and the exhilarated laughter and voices of people being refreshed by the cool water. Fall sees the birds return on their way south as small animals prepare for winter, and summertime residents close up their houses.

Right *Although Fire Island is a popular summer retreat, great effort has been made to preserve the natural life here. The salt marshes are home to many species of wildfowl.*

Below *Summertime residents have fled back to the cities leaving Fire Island National Park to the wildfowl and the fog for the winter.*

Above   *Davis Park Marina on Fire Island provides a berth for all manner of small craft.*

Assateague Island National Seashore

The great barrier islands of the Atlantic have long been subject to tropical hurricanes that have shaped and reshaped their boundaries. We take particular notice today, for each storm that travels the coast makes news across the nation, and, whether or not one has experienced the fury of a "Hazel" or a "Connie" or a "Diane," there is a sense of despair at the loss of life and property. One wonders, too, in reading of the extraordinary wind speeds and tide elevations — or seeing, as cameras all too readily focus on such disasters — what nature has in store for the next visit.

The worst storm in the twentieth century struck the Atlantic Coast in 1962, and it was that storm that in a large part brought about the establishment of Assateague Island as a national seashore.

In 1935, the Department of the Interior conducted a survey of unspoiled Atlantic seashores that could still be saved for public enjoyment. Assateague Island, a narrow, 37-mile-long stem of sand and marsh belonging to both Maryland and Virginia, had all the basic features to qualify, but 15 miles of it had already been developed; it was too late. More than 3000 private owners had moved in through the years and built summer cottages and houses. Then came the storm of '62. When that "extratropical" storm of cyclone proportions had its way, there seemed little left for human habitation. Property

Below *From one decade to the next, Assateague Island National Seashore changes — in the past 30 years the island has moved 1000 feet closer to the mainland under the influence of the sea.*

was purchased and the congressional act establishing Assateague Island National Seashore was signed into law on August 25, 1965, by President Lyndon B. Johnson.

Like other barrier islands along the Atlantic Coast, Assateague hardly retains its appearance from one century to the next — perhaps even from one decade or one year to the next. Sometimes the changes can be dramatic. For example, it is estimated that Assateague has moved westward toward the mainland by 1000 feet in the past 30 years. Such manifestations of nature's forces are not always so visible, but for those who watch closely, the evidence is clear. Barrier island life is at the mercy of the sea. The Atlantic made Assateague; it is the Atlantic that shapes it; and, someday, it will be the Atlantic that will take it away.

Assateague Island is best known for its ponies. Legend has it that the ancestors of the wild ponies that roam Assateague and Chincoteague National Wildlife Refuge (75 per cent of the ponies are at the refuge) came from the wreck of a Spanish galleon around 1821 or so. They were small horses purposefully blinded for use in mines, and these were being sent home after working in Central America. There were already horses on Assateague, sent out to pasture by colonists as early as the mid-seventeenth-century. The two bred. Today's ponies are still smaller than horses, shaggy, and quite sturdy, to say nothing of still being wild.

Above *Assateague's wild ponies are smaller than horses, shaggy and quite sturdy, and true to their name they remain untamed.*

CAPE HATTERAS NATIONAL SEASHORE

When in 1524 the Italian navigator Giovanni da Verrazano reported to the King of France, his royal employer, that he had discovered an isthmus separating the Atlantic and Pacific oceans, he had actually seen only the Outer Banks of North Carolina, so wide was the sound beyond which the mainland was invisible. Unlike Fire Island and Assateague, which hug the New York and Maryland shores so closely, the Carolina Outer Banks curve out to the sea as much as 30 miles to form a 175-mile-long bulging chain of narrow islands from the Virginia border just south of Norfolk to Cape Lookout. Constantly and erratically widening and narrowing, the Outer Banks, barely a mile wide in some places, have become one of the East's favorite playgrounds.

Like Cape Cod when first discovered, the Outer Banks were forested with cedar, pine, and oak when John White, leader of Roanoke Island's "Lost Colony," drew his 1585 map. And like the Massachusetts Pilgrims, the settlers who followed White brought with them axes and cattle, and soon Cape Hatteras too became long islands of shifting sand dunes no longer anchored by vegetation and trees.

What man did not destroy, the violence of the coastal storms did. The Outer Banks were born of violence. The islands yield to storms and hurricanes; gigantic waves lash out at the banks and into the sound, and then back again to sea; what little vegetation is there is blasted with sand, tree trunks covered, dunes blown and scattered. Well off at sea, the southern and northern ocean currents meet in unbridled collision, sending giant swells into the air and toward the shores, stirring underwater sands into huge, menacing ridges called shoals. At Diamond Shoals, 12 miles directly off Cape Hatteras, more than 600 ships, including the Civil War's *Monitor*, are known to have been wrecked and hundreds of lives lost on these hazardous underwater ranges of sand and in the terrifying storms that create them. Thousands of other ships of all sizes and shapes lie buried along Carolina's coast, more than could possibly be documented, christening this stretch of water the "Graveyard of the Atlantic".

Cape Hatteras is at the sea's edge, but no well-defined boundary marks precisely where the sea ends and the land begins. Here land and sea work together in an uneasy alliance. They share many valuable resources. But the sea rules the barrier islands.

Right *Evidence of early colonization on this Cape Hatteras sand and shingle spit can be seen in the top left of the picture. The lighthouse (see inset) warns navigators of the dangerous shoals which lie just off the spit.*

Below *More than 600 ships are known to have been shipwrecked off Cape Hatteras, at Diamond Shoals, on treacherous sandbars created by violent storms. This part of Carolina's coastline is called the "Graveyard of the Atlantic" with good cause. The bare bones of one of these ships lie half-exposed in the sands on Hatteras.*

CANAVERAL NATIONAL SEASHORE

In the early 1960s, the Kennedy Space Center was established on part of Merritt Island, another of the Atlantic's barrier islands — that general area so often called Cape Canaveral, Florida. Not all the land was needed for the space program, and so two other government agencies were invited to help manage the area. In 1963, the Fish and Wildlife Service, in cooperation with NASA, established the Merritt Island National Wildlife Refuge as a sanctuary for wintering waterfowl. With the creation of Canaveral National Seashore in 1975, the National Park Service took on the dual responsibility of preserving the primitive barrier beach while providing for public enjoyment of its resources. Thus three different governmental agencies have joined to ensure the proper mesh of the nation's highly technical space program, wildlife management, and public recreation.

Like all the other barrier islands to the north, Merritt Island is subject to the powers of wind, water, and shifting sands. The landscape is different; hammocks of ancient oak trees draped with Spanish moss grow within walking distance of palmetto-covered sand dunes; salt marshes, man-made impoundments, mangrove islands, and the estuaries of lagoon and river serve as feeding grounds for an array of sub-tropical wildlife. Birdlife abounds on Merritt Island, with more than 180 species recorded. Both the seashore and the refuge are located beneath the Atlantic Flyway, the major migratory route for birds between their southern wintering grounds and northern breeding areas.

The Kennedy Space Center shares Merritt Island with the seashore and the refuge — or is it the other way around — and on occasion provides its own special thing to American culture. It is said that the wildlife is not disturbed, and perhaps not. Preservation is still the goal. So far, it seems to be working.

Right Discovery *shares Cape Canaveral with wintering waterfowl. Not all the land on Merritt Island is needed for the space program, so NASA cooperates with the Fish and Wildlife Service and the National Park Service to provide a sanctuary for waterfowl and a recreation area for the public.*

Below *Waterfowl at a dried up pond, seen against the Kennedy Space Center.*

EVERGLADES NATIONAL PARK

The Everglades, at the southern-most tip of Florida, is not a barrier island or a national seashore or a vast monument set aside simply for the enjoyment of the public. As Grand Canyon National Park locks the geological past into a protective state for all to see, Everglades National Park bounds forever the nation's most significant, and perhaps most fragile, natural scene. Within these precious 1 400 000 subtropical acres is the most complex and delicately balanced of all the planet's relationships: life, from the lowest biological organism to the alligator, and its never-ending chain of prey and predator; and another relationship with the intruder, man.

The ecosystem of the Everglades can be likened to the thin shell of a bird's egg, so fragile that the slightest crack will do irreparable harm. Probably no other natural area in the National Park System, perhaps in the whole of the country, is so delicately balanced between survival and destruction as the Everglades. And it has been abused by man and his follies more than any other. If we ever lose a national park, it will be the

Right *The Everglades is a limestone basin lined with layers of peat and decaying plant life — the Ten Thousand Islands float in this basin slowing the pace of the river even further.*

Below *Thanks to the Audubon Society and other conservation organizations, beautiful tropical birds like this roseate spoonbill are now returning in healthy numbers to Everglades National Park.*

Everglades, not because of development, but from the tipping of the ecological scales.

The Everglades is a broad, flat river of fresh water that flows from Lake Okeechobee in central Florida, 120 miles south to Florida Bay and the Gulf of Mexico. The endless "river of grass" moves so slowly that it seems to not move at all. The life it once harbored may have been the most abundant anywhere, so lush and conducive is its climate to everything that lives. But even then, nature had to cling tenaciously to a shallow foothold.

The southern tip of Florida is low country; the highest point in the state is only 345 feet, and that's in the northern panhandle. At the Everglades, land is measured in inches. It was not always like this. Several times in the past one million years, the sea level between glacial periods left this peninsula of ancient limestone high and dry. As the glaciers melted, the land was flooded. Ridges of limestone were built around the perimeters, thus creating a shallow bowl in the present shape of the state.

The Everglades, then, is more than just the river of grass; it is a limestone basin,

tilted slightly to the south and west, and lined with layers of peat and decayed plant life that collects about 60 inches of rainfall each year. That is what it is supposed to be. Some changes have been made in the past 70 years that have seriously jeopardized this wonderland.

Florida was inhabited by Indians since the 1500s, and Seminoles, off-shoots of the nineteenth century Creek Confederation, still survive here. But the white man discovered Florida around the turn of the century and it has not been the same since. One of his "discoveries" was that the Everglades could be farmed by drawing water off the thin layer of rich topsoil. Dikes were laid around Lake Okeechobee and canals were built to drain the fresh water off to the sea. But something went wrong. The lake flooded and spilled and thousands of people died. The project failed. The fine organic soil they had uncovered oxidized and the peat base burned. Salt water filtered in to fill the vacuum and the Everglades began to dry up in the drought season. The whole fragile ecosystem of southern Florida was turned upside down.

The land was not the only victim of human greed. Once the Everglades was the

Inset *The climate of the Everglades is lush but the ecological balance is a delicate one even for the grasshoppers that cling to the rivers of swamp grass.*

home of thousands of beautiful tropical birds. Around 1886, early settlers found that there was a healthy market for feathers. The New York millinery industry paid handsomely for plumes for ladies' hats. Before the hunters were done, herons and egrets had nearly disappeared. The Audubon Society and other conservation organizations banded together to protect the birds, the rapidly diminishing alligator, and other wildlife, and, in fact, to save the Everglades as a park. In 1916, a small section was set aside as a state park. Everglades National Park was authorized in 1934 and was formally established in 1947.

Life still hangs by a thread in this elegant but fragile land. The boundaries came too late, and persistent progress still hammers away at the edges, but some ecosystems are slowly returning and some wildlife may come back. No one should expect miracles. The importance and uniqueness of the Everglades ecosystems have now been recognized by its designation as an International Biosphere Reserve and as a World Heritage Site. But it will take human concern and prudent management to preserve the park's natural treasures.

Left *Around the turn of the century, attempts were made, with disastrous results, to drain parts of the Everglades in order to farm the thin layer of rich top soil. The fragile ecosystem was greatly disturbed and some of the areas including Everglade Lake struggle continuously to recover this ecological balance.*

Below and left *In Big Cypress Swamp, alligator flag flowers at the foot of cypress trees (see left) draped in Spanish Moss.*

Bottom *The rapidly diminishing alligator is now protected in Everglades National Park along with other birds and wildlife, in the hope that these animals will return in greater numbers to the Everglades.*

BISCAYNE NATIONAL PARK

Biscayne National Park, just 21 miles east of Everglades National Park, is one of the newest national parks in the conterminous states (1980), and is, without doubt, one of the most delightful and charming areas within the entire system. Composed of a large mainland mangrove shoreline, shallow and warm Biscayne Bay, the islands or keys, and the coral reefs, the park bounds a 175 000 acre subtropical setting of terrestrial and undersea life into a recreational paradise. The water is refreshingly clean, extraordinarily clear, and filled with a dazzling array of exotic tropical fish — the stoplight parrotfish, goosehead scorpionfish, princess venus, finger garlic sponge, peppermint goby — and a kaleidoscope of brilliantly colored and intricately designed coral reef. A Caribbean-like climate provides the year-round sunshine and abundant rainfall in which tropical life of all kinds thrives — lush green forests of flowers, shrubs, ferns, vines, and trees.

Biscayne is not a barrier island as is Cape Hatteras and Cumberland Island, but it is a pleasant link in the chain that moves around to Gulf Islands National Seashore.

Below *Flamingoes wade and feed in warm and shallow Biscayne Bay, just 21 miles east of Everglades National Park.*

Left *Biscayne National Park has a number of islands or keys within the boundaries of the park. It also includes a section of mainland shoreline, Biscayne Bay and coral reefs, taking in some 175 000 acres.*

Both below *The extraordinarily clear, clean water of Biscayne Bay is home to a dazzling array of tropical fish like this Soldier Fish, and a kaleidoscope of brilliantly colored coral like this Acropora variabilis.*

THE GULF OF MEXICO is virtually an inland sea. Its warm and gentle waters have nurtured a 1600 mile paradise of broad marshes and swamps, along the Florida, Alabama, Mississippi, and Louisiana coasts, and wild, sandy beaches reminiscent of the Outer Banks along the east coast of Texas. Subject to monstrous storms that sometimes devastate all life forms, and man-made pollutants that blacken beaches and kill everything in their wake, the environment seemingly recovers quickly and once again becomes "a center of life," as John Muir called the Gulf.

Below *A dramatic view of the Mississippi River Delta at New Orleans, before it reaches the Gulf of Mexico.*

Gulf Island National Seashore

Here in the northeastern Gulf of Mexico, the U.S. Congress has set aside several of the barrier islands for recreation and for their natural and historical resources. The seashore stretches from the east end of Santa Rosa Island in Florida, 150 miles west to West Ship Island in Mississippi. (The intervening islands in Alabama are not a part of the park.) But there is more to this place than just the islands. Some mainland areas have been designated a part of the seashore as well: old forts dating back to the Civil War, an experimental tree farm started by John Quincy Adams, archeological traces of the earliest inhabitants, and the plants and wildlife of the estuaries, those arms of the sea where saltwater and freshwater mix.

The barrier islands, however, are the glue that holds this mosaic of land and water together. The source of the brilliant white sand is rock material from the upland regions to the north. Over millions of years, streams and rivers moved the weathered remains of these rocks down to the sea.

These islands are ever-changing, moving constantly to the west. Littoral currents wear away the eastern ends and build up the western ends. Violent storms cause overwash that rearranges large amounts of sand. Change by the winds is slowed only by the protective covering of grasses and other vegetation growing on the dune line nearest the gulf. The elaborate stem and root system of the sea oat, in particular, is vital to the protection and stabilization of barrier islands. So important, in fact, that the picking or disturbing of sea oats and other vegetation is strictly prohibited.

Below *The deep-rooted sea oats form a barrier against the brilliant shifting white sands.*

PADRE ISLAND NATIONAL SEASHORE

Curving concavely along the eastern coast of Texas, from Galveston south to Brownsville, is a 350-mile-long series of barrier islands creating bays and sounds and lagoons and seaports. Several wildlife refuges dot the coast, but, with one major exception, the islands are unprotected. That exception is one of the jewels in the National Park System — Padre Island National Seashore. Beginning at Corpus Christi, and pointing south toward Mexico, is a slender, 113-mile-long, fragile piece of Texas real estate that is as filled with legends of lost treasures as it is modern debris from the sea. On any given day, the endless beach and glorious sky of Padre Island belie the turbulent history which has surrounded the barrier in modern times — devastating hurricanes, oil spills washed ashore, and human encroachment that have threatened its existence.

Established as a national seashore in 1968, it is one of the newer protected areas in the National Park System, but its history goes back to the early sixteenth century when it was discovered by Spaniards and named Las Islas Blancas, the White Islands.

Padre Island National Seashore is a textbook example of a barrier island — wide, clean beaches of sand that give way to small shells; next, dunes paralleling the shore, then grassy flats broken up by smaller dunes which finally give way to sand dunes and mudflats merging with the lagoon waters.

Many Spanish galleons saw their end along these shores, not the least of which was a fleet of ships loaded with gold that was wrecked here in a 1553 storm that still haunts treasure seekers. Later the island was named Padre after Padre Nicholas Balli, who took possession in 1800 on a land grant and began grazing cattle.

Padre Island ranges in width from about a few hundred yards to three miles, and is separated from the mainland by Laguna Madre, a shallow body of water with a maximum width of ten miles. The national seashore encompasses the undeveloped central section of the island, 80.5 miles long.

From gulf to lagoon, the island consists of a wide, clean beach of sand that in places gives way to small shells; next an alignment of dunes paralleling the shore; then grassy flats, broken here and there by smaller dunes; and last a vaguely defined area of sand dunes and mudflats that merges with the lagoon waters. In short, Padre is a textbook example of a barrier island, formed in the same way as the others, delicate as the others, its human history very much similar. There may be three major differences: it is warmer, there are more reptiles here than on the other barriers, and…it's in Texas.

THE COASTAL PARKS OF THE PACIFIC are as different from the Atlantic seashores as Acadia is from the Everglades, indeed as different as California's Channel Islands are from the Redwood forests and the glacial bays to the north. The western coast of the United States, from Baja California to British Columbia, is nearly 8000 miles of shoreline facing a sharp dropoff of up to 12 000 feet to the ocean floor. While the eastern edge of the continent slopes off gently and shows signs of sinking into the sea, the eroded cliffs of the western shores resemble the remnants of vast mountains. The Channel Islands, off the coast of Southern California, for example, are indeed the peaks of mountains faulted downward. There is still much geological activity going on. Plate tectonics theories have warned scientists that the great folding of floating mantles will inexorably alter the coastal states in the future. Movements along the San Andreas Fault, the eruption of Mt. Saint Helens…nature is not done with the Pacific "ring of fire."

Below *The wildlife along the coastal parks of the Pacific is rich not only in numbers but in species — from the microscopic to the monumental. This Californian brown pelican waits to feed upon the bounty of the waters.*

34

Cabrillo National Monument

Fifty years after Columbus landed in the New World, Juan Rodriguez Cabrillo set out on his epic voyage of discovery. Commanding two small ships of sail, he braved "great storms of rain, heavy clouds, great darkness, and heavy air" as he ranged into unknown waters, into *ne plus ultra* — no more beyond. For the glory of God and the promise of riches Cabrillo's expedition explored the entire length of the California coast, taking possession in the name of the King of Spain and the Viceroy of Mexico. Cabrillo National Monument commemorates the landing site of the Spanish sailor — he named the "closed and very good" harbor San Miguel. It is now San Diego.

This small historic site — the Old Point Loma Lighthouse and a fine visitor center — is really far more than just an extraordinary site for viewing the San Diego harbor. On the western — Pacific — side of Point Loma is even better scenery. A visit in late December or January, or perhaps February, will be in time for the annual migration of the California Gray Whale. Each year, as they have perhaps for thousands or millions of years, the whales pass Point Loma on their way from the Arctic Ocean to the lagoons of Baja, California. They leave their summer feeding grounds in the Bering and Chukchi Seas in late September when the surface begins to freeze. Their 5000 mile journey takes them to the sheltered waters of Scammons Lagoon and Magdalene Bay, where the pregnant females bear their calves.

Just below Point Loma, where the ocean meets the land, is a rocky environment of marine plants and animals that have adapted to harsh tidal conditions. These tidepools are host to the flowery anemone, the scavenging lineshore crab, grazing limpets, spongy dead man's fingers, and a hundred other species of plants and animals.

Cabrillo is small, yet a diversified park; one of the most pleasant in the system. From here you can see the U.S. Naval Base in San Diego harbor, you can see the city itself, or, if you really want to look for them, and it's a clear day, you can see the mountains of the desert a hundred miles away.

Left and bottom *In the sheltered waters around Cabrillo, California Gray Whales bear their calves. One gray whale surfaces in the "spy" position, then displays its fluke before diving.*

Below *A grand view of San Diego Harbor can be had not far from the Old Point Loma Lighthouse — an historic site within Cabrillo National Monument.*

CHANNEL ISLANDS NATIONAL PARK

The Channel Islands, an island chain lying just off California's southern coast, appear quite close to land on clear days. Five of the eight islands and their surrounding six nautical miles of ocean comprise Channel Islands National Park and National Marine Sanctuary. In 1980, Congress designated Anacapa, Santa Cruz, Santa Rosa, San Miguel, and Santa Barbara Islands, and 125 000 acres of submerged lands as a national park because they possess outstanding and unique natural and cultural resources. The National Marine Sanctuary was established later that year. The park and sanctuary provide habitat for marine life ranging from microscopic plankton to the largest creature on earth — the blue whale.

Channel Islands National Park is part of the International Man and the Biosphere program to conserve genetic diversity and an environmental baseline for research and monitoring throughout the world.

Below *One of the Channel Islands designated a national park in 1980, Santa Barbara is a habitat for birds and marine life.*

POINT REYES NATIONAL SEASHORE

The Point Reyes Peninsula is an unusual, dislocated land which has long puzzled geologists. Rocks of this craggy shore match those of the Tehachapi Mountains more than 300 miles to the south. When the theory of plate tectonics was accepted in scientific circles, geologists had their explanation — continental drift, the constant motion of the earth's crust. The Point Reyes Peninsula rides high on the eastern edge of the Pacific plate. This, one of the six great plates forming most of the earth's crust, creeps steadily northwestward about three inches a year. The rest of North America, except Alaska, is borne westward on the slower-moving American plate.

Here in Olema Valley, near the park headquarters, these two great land masses grind together. Where one plate ends and another begins cannot be pinpointed accurately, for a single fault line does not exist. This meeting of the plates is, quite simply, a rift zone, which contains many large and small faults running parallel and at odd angles to one another. Because each plate cannot move freely, tremendous pressures build up along this junction. The jumbled nature of the surface landscape is the manifestation of stress far below the surface of the earth, often as much as 250 miles deep. From time to time this pressure becomes too great and the underlying rock breaks loose with dramatic and sometimes catastrophic results and the land surface itself actually moves. This is what happened in the Olema Valley in 1906; the result was the devastating San Francisco earthquake. At this time, the Point Reyes Peninsula was thrust 16.4 feet northwestward.

The peaceful landscape of Point Reyes belies what goes on beneath. Streams and estuaries cut through the folded hills and valleys; miles of beaches are within sight of Douglas fir and bishop pine forests; deer browse near rocks, sea lions bask in the sun.

Inset An ancient rock surface of fossils lies exposed at Drake's Bay in Point Reyes National Seashore. According to the now accepted theory of plate tectonics, two great land masses grind together here, creating a rift zone of many small and large faults.

Below Miles of rocky beaches lined with peaceful Douglas fir and pine forests belie the turmoil that goes on beneath the surface of this beautiful stretch of seashore.

OLYMPIC NATIONAL PARK

The shores of Oregon and Washington, unlike those of California, are remnants of ancient mountains and headlands long eroded by the ceaseless pounding of the Pacific waves. Beaches are narrow with high, rugged cliffs and lush rain forests behind, and the environment at the water's edge extends inland some 30 miles to influence the abundant wildlife and plant growth into the Olympic Mountains. Sand beaches are few along these shores; the shores are mostly rocky, the waters cold. There are caves, sandspits, and pinnacles of rock called seastacks, remnants of ancient headlands worn away by the constant waves.

While the entire Olympic National Park is a part of the coastal mountain range, there is a narrow, 50-mile-long strip along the water's edge that is separated from the main park land. There are no barrier islands. The Pacific Ocean, unchecked for 5000 miles, pounds relentlessly against these shores — two tons per square inch, it has been estimated. It builds and tears away at the same time in a never-ending contest of force and strength. Waves as high as 200 feet lash the cliffs as the sea rises and recedes.

Far right *Rain forests of Douglas fir, moss-hung cedar, ferns and bracken thrive on the moisture-laden fogs along the Pacific coast of Olympic National Park.*

Right *Rocky beaches and high cliffs take relentless punishment from the waves of the Pacific Ocean. Worn by the action of these waves, seastacks like this one at Cape Alava stand as the remnants of some ancient headland.*

Below *Olympic National Park extends inland to the heavily-forested and snow-capped Olympic Mountains which run along the Oregon and Washington coast.*

GLACIER BAY NATIONAL PARK

On July 9, 1958, an earthquake along Alaska's Fairweather fault caused the release of 90 million tons of rock and soil into the head of Lituya Bay in Glacier Bay National Park. A wall of water 1700 feet high rose on the other side of the bay, scraping off every tree in its path. Displaced water, traveling at the rate of 150 miles an hour, surged into the bay seven miles away taking with it forests on both sides.

The recorded history of glacial activity along the Alaskan coast suggests that this may be the wildest of all our coastlands, and that, indeed, there is much more to come. As the earth's crust continues to fold, the change from peaceful scenery to violent upheaval can be sudden. The comings and goings of glaciers also have effects on the sea level and land surface. As they slowly move toward the coast and melt into the ocean, the earth's water mass rises. It is estimated that the Wisconsinan Ice Age sea level was 325 feet lower than it is today. At the same time, glaciers sometimes more than a mile thick — depress the bedrock. As the glaciers melt, the land slowly rebounds. As a result, in some places in Alaska, the United States is growing at the rate of one-and-a-half inches of new land a year.

In 1879, JOHN MUIR, the great naturalist who was so responsible for our early conservation movements, traveled to Alaska and asked to see an "ice mountain" he had heard about. He described what later was to be named for him:

> AT LENGTH THE CLOUDS LIFTED A LITTLE, AND BENEATH THEIR GRAY FRINGES I SAW THE BERG-FILLED EXPANSE OF THE BAY, AND THE FEET OF THE MOUNTAINS THAT STAND ABOUT IT, AND THE IMPOSING FRONTS OF FIVE HUGE GLACIERS, THE NEAREST BEING IMMEDIATELY BENEATH ME. THIS WAS MY FIRST GENERAL VIEW OF GLACIER BAY, A SOLITUDE OF ICE AND SNOW AND NEWBORN ROCKS, DIM, DREARY, MYSTERIOUS …BREASTING THE SNOW AGAIN, CROSSING THE SHIFTING AVALANCHE SLOPES AND TORRENTS, I REACHED CAMP ABOUT DARK, WET AND WEARY…AND GLAD.

The snow- and ice-covered mountains of the Fairweather Range are as impressive as the glaciers of this park. The highest peak is 15 320-foot Mount Fairweather. Several other summits, including Mounts Crillon, Quincy Adams, La Perouse, Lituya, Salisbury, and Root, exceed 10 000 feet. The steepness of their slopes is dramatically

Right A river of ice flowing down the mountains into Glacier Bay, this glacier may shift great quantities of meltwater and debris in its path.

Below The St Elias Mountains towering above Glacier Bay National Park, Alaska record the comings and goings of not-so-ancient glaciers in their furrows and basins.

visible throughout the upper bay. In Johns Hopkins Inlet, several peaks rise from sea level to 6000 feet within four miles of the shore. The peaks supply moisture to all glaciers on the peninsula separating Glacier Bay from the Gulf of Alaska.

Before the last glacial advance, much of the land in the upper bay was covered by forests of spruce and hemlock. With the forward movement of the glaciers came great quantities of meltwater and debris. The shifting streams flooded and then buried the trees under many feet of sand and gravel. Glaciers then advanced over the sediments and for perhaps 3000 years the forests lay buried. As glaciers melted, their outwash streams cut through the deep deposits and exposed the ancient stumps, many still in upright position.

Life quickly reinvades the land recently covered with ice. As late as 1700, Glacier Bay was covered with an icecap 3000 feet thick, but the ice front was retreating even as John Muir wrote his words. The Muir Glacier has retreated 30 miles since 1879. And as all these giant sheets of ice slowly withdraw, the jagged Alaska Coast of the United States grows.

Below *Life invades land recently uncovered by ice. As the glaciers retreat, vegetation grasps a foothold and the jagged coast of Alaska slowly grows.*

Left *The movement of the glaciers causes great crevasses to appear — this one on the Brooks Range side of Glacier Bay.*

Below *A massive wall of blue ice pushes relentlessly into the sea, creating icebergs as the walls collapse into the water.*

Thus Ever the Land and Sea are Changing

NOW WE HAVE CANYON GORGES AND DEEPLY ERODED VALLEYS,
AND STILL THE HILLS ARE DISAPPEARING,
THE MOUNTAINS THEMSELVES ARE WASTING AWAY, PLATEAUS ARE DISSOLVING,
AND THE GEOLOGIST, IN THE LIGHT OF THE PAST HISTORY OF THE EARTH,
MAKES PROPHECY OF A TIME WHEN THIS DESOLATE LAND OF TITANIC ROCKS
SHALL BECOME A VALLEY OF MANY VALLEYS, AND YET AGAIN
THE SEA WILL INVADE THE LAND, AND THE CORAL ANIMALS BUILD THEIR REEFS...
THUS EVER THE LAND AND SEA ARE CHANGING;
OLD LANDS ARE BURIED, AND NEW LANDS ARE BORN.

JOHN WESLEY POWELL
Explorations of the Canyons of the Colorado

There is no landscape on this planet more awesome, more spectacular, than the Colorado Plateau of the American Southwest, the most revealing single piece of the earth's geological roots. It begins at Dinosaur National Monument, straddling the Utah and Colorado border, where the Green River cuts through the Uintah Mountains and flows south into the desert and canyon country to rendezvous in Canyonlands National Park with the Colorado River running southwest from the Rocky Mountains. The boundary — there is no real boundary of the Colorado Plateau — encompasses the Four Corners Country, parts of Utah, Colorado, Arizona, and New Mexico and includes eight national parks: Arches, Capitol Reef, Canyonlands, Mesa Verde, Petrified Forest, Bryce Canyon, Zion, and Grand Canyon, as well as 19 other monuments and recreation areas.

The plateau is a mile above sea level, but it is believed that at various times in geological history it was submerged below water, perhaps as many as seven times before the seas withdrew. Each one of these periods deposited vast layers of sediments that later solidified into rock — mostly sandstone. When the land was raised and pushed together by what geologists now believe to be a floating of the earth's crust on fluid mantles, the Rockies were formed, sending great rivers and streams toward the ocean, carving out canyons and mesas as they went. Millions of years of erosion have left the spectacular landscape of the "Red Rock Country", or "Standing Up Country", as it is sometimes called — "Standing Up" because there is more rock standing than lying down.

While water created the Colorado Plateau, the lack of it has left a desert. Still rivers and streams continue to cut through the canyons in a ceaseless erosion that is constantly changing — literally from one day to the next — the shape of the plateau. The Colorado River is the main force that drains some 90 per cent of the plateau area as it rushes southwest toward the Gulf of California. Its muddy-red waters meet the Green River in Canyonlands National Park, near Moab, Utah. Feeding into it from all sides are the Yampa, White, Gunnison, Fremont, Delores, Escalante, San Juan, Virgin, Juan, and a dozen other major and minor tributaries. Combined, they are a tremendous force, an erosive power unlike anywhere else in North America.

The carving of the Grand Canyon is the work of rains and rivers — the mightiest of these is the Colorado River which cuts through the Canyon here at Toroweap Overlook.

CANYONLANDS NATIONAL PARK

This is a land that took 300 million years to build; sandstone from oceans, winds, floods, and eroded mountains, each with its own effect, each in its own time. But time passes slowly here; change is imperceptible. Canyonlands — or that national park called Canyonlands, for, indeed, all of this is the land of canyons — is a rough rectangle approximately 35 miles long and 20 miles wide at the heart of the Colorado Plateau. With the exception of the Grand Canyon, further on down the Colorado River, it is one of the most breath-taking and geologically important areas of the nation. It is made up of four main sections: the Island in the Sky, a 6000-foot mesa dominating the region between the Colorado and Green rivers; the two rivers and their canyons; the Maze District to the west; and the Needles area to the south. In and around these is a blazing mass of deep canyons, valleys, and basins, extraordinary buttes, mesas, towers, domes, knobs, fins, arches, and caves, and hundreds of red-rock and sandstone formations at once frightening and beautiful.

The Colorado and its major tributary, the Green River, are responsible for this sweeping landscape, cutting through the rock and stripping away, bit by bit for millions of years, the plateau and walls. Grandview Point, a finger of the Island in the Sky pointing south toward the confluence of the two rivers is, indeed, a view of the grandest proportions, but from here the rivers are mere streams, twisting and turning through the gorges, disappearing at times, shining in the bright sunlight around this bend and that. To the west of Grandview lies the Green River flowing placidly south from Wyoming; across it can be seen the Land of the Standing Rocks and the Maze; to the south the Colorado and the confluence with the Green, and farther on, the Needles; the grand, snow-capped La Sal mountains rise off to the east; and immediately below, terraced toward the rivers, the White Rim, some 1000 feet down, with still another 1000-foot-drop to the basin. The vastness of the place is staggering; the feeling of openness — the broad, clear skies, the sound of wind and the occasional cry of a bird — is magnificent.

Freeman Tilden — who wrote so much about the parks — described Canyonlands as the place where "the adjective died of exhaustion". Even he was at a loss for words.

Right *From the air, the vastness of Canyonlands is staggering; the feeling of openness, the broad clear skies, the sweep of the landscape remind the viewer that this land was 300 million years in the making.*

Below *Canyonlands National Park from Dead Horse Point, Utah, is a blazing mass of deep canyons, valleys, extraordinary buttes as well as hundreds of red-rock and sandstone formations.*

ARCHES NATIONAL PARK

A short distance north of Canyonlands National Park is the greatest density of natural arches in the world, a small park — by comparison to Canyonlands — that lies on the north bank of the Colorado River near Moab, Utah. Wind and water, extreme temperatures, and underground salt movements have sculpted this magnificent scenery, so delicately formed that one marvels at its stability, fearing to trample lest the arches crack and fall to the ground. On serene, clear days, it is hard to imagine that 100 million years of sandstone erosion created this land. The more than 200 catalogued arches range in size from a three-foot opening, the minimum considered an arch, to Landscape Arch, the longest in the world, a 105-foot high ribbon of rock measuring 291 feet from base to base.

All stages of arch formation and decay can be found here. Delicate Arch, an isolated remnant of a bygone fin, stands on the brink of a canyon, with the white-capped La Sal Mountains in the background. Spires and pinnacles and balanced rocks perched atop seemingly inadequate bases vie with the arches as scenic spectacles. Early explorers thought the huge arches and monoliths in the Windows Section of the park were, like Stonehenge in England, works of some lost culture.

The facts are that the park lies atop an underground salt bed, which is basically responsible for the formations. Thousands of feet thick in places, this salt bed was

Previous page   Like the Grand Canyon, further on down the Colorado River, Canyonlands has been shaped by the river, as it cut through rock and stripped away, bit by bit for a million years, the plateaus and walls.

Previous page inset   Near Moab, many smaller rivers and streams continue to cut through the canyons, constantly eroding the landscape, literally transforming the shape of the plateau.

deposited over the Colorado Plateau some 300 million years ago. Over countless eons, the salt bed was covered with residue from floods and winds and the oceans that came at intervals. Much of the covering debris was compressed into rock. The earth covering Arches may have been as much as one mile thick.

Salt is unstable, and the salt bed below Arches was no match for the weight of this thick cover of rock. Under such pressure it shifted, buckled, liquified, and repositioned itself, thrusting the earth layers upward into domes. Whole sections dropped into cavities. In places they turned almost on edge. Faults occurred. The result of one such 2500 foot displacement, the Moab Fault, can be seen from the park visitor center.

As this subsurface movement of salt shaped the earth, surface erosion stripped away the younger rock layers. Except for isolated remnants, the major formations visible in Arches today are the salmon-colored Entrada Sandstone, in which most of the arches form, and the buff-colored Navajo sandstone. These are placed in layer-cake fashion through most of the park. Over time the superficial cracks, joints, and folds of these layers were saturated with water. Ice formed in the fissures, melted under extreme desert heat, and winds cleaned out the loose particles. A series of free-standing fins remained. Wind and water attacked these fins until, in some, the cementing material gave way and chunks of rock tumbled out. Many damaged fins collapsed. Others, with the right degree of hardness and balance, survived despite their missing middles. These became the arches we see today.

Below *Wind and water, extreme temperatures and underground salt movements have sculpted the more than 200 catalogued arches in Arches National Park. Ranging in size from a 3-foot opening to something the size of Landscape Arch — a 105-foot high ribbon measuring 291 feet from base to base, it is possible to track all the stages of arch formation and decay here in the park.*

BRYCE CANYON NATIONAL PARK

Ebeneezer Bryce lived here for five years in the late 1870s and tried to make a living. When he gave up, he left his name and an apt description. Said he, "A hell of a place to lose a cow!" Paiute Indians fared little better than Bryce. They called it *Unka-timpe-wa-wince-pock-ich:* "Red rocks standing like men in a bowl-shaped canyon." If all of this implies that Bryce Canyon defies description, it may well be true, but only in that it changes so often. True, it may well have been hostile country for farming, but then early settlers were hardly looking for beauty. If Bryce saw anything else in the canyon besides his cows, he did not tell us. The Paiutes, on the other hand, had a slightly different perspective. We know precious little about them other than the spiritual values they seemed to attach to the odd formations that make up this park. Their name for Bryce rings of superstition, and no doubt its origins are in the legend that the Indian's ancestors were sinful folk who in defying the gods were turned to stone.

The first white men to come into this southwestern corner of Utah were two Spanish priests, Dominguez and Escalante, in 1776, the year Benjamin Franklin and Thomas Jefferson were proposing independence more than 2000 miles away in Philadelphia, Pennsylvania. The two priests were searching for an easy route from Santa Fe, New Mexico, to Monterey, California. They missed Bryce and Zion canyons, as did Jedediah Smith, who ventured this way 50 years later in search of beaver pelts. There seems little doubt that early Mormon settlers were the first to see Bryce. Their pioneer villages sprang up all around the canyon. By 1923, Bryce Canyon National Monument had been established; it became a national park five years later.

In the overall scheme of things on the Colorado Plateau, Bryce Canyon has played less of a role than other parks. It is not a canyon, and no major river has carved its formations. Rather is Bryce Canyon an amphitheater eroded out of the side of a plateau by thousands of rain-fed rivulets over millions of years. Water, in the form of heavy rains, snow, and ice, has in all probability been the exclusive erosive agent. Where Grand Canyon has been carved and cut out, Bryce has been literally washed away.

What remains are innumerable bizarre pinnacles, walls and spires of highly colored hue. Bryce Canyon National Park is an area with the most unusual erosional forms in the world.

Next page   More like an amphitheater than a canyon, Bryce has been eroded out of the side of the plateau by a million years of rain, snow, and ice.

Right   A natural bridge formed by countless tributaries and streams in Bryce.

Below   "Red rocks standing like men in a bowl-shaped canyon" was the description accorded to Bryce Canyon by Paiute Indians.

Zion National Park

Zion Canyon was cut by the Virgin River in southwestern Utah, and like other areas of the Plateau, the erosional effects of rain, wind, and frost, has continued the process of forming another extraordinary pocket of beauty just 90 miles from Bryce Canyon. The Virgin rages on, and to this day carries on toward the Colorado — for it is the largest tributary in southern Utah — hundreds of thousands of tons of rock each year. The amazing thing is that this can be seen.

Placid at times, the Virgin River can rage during replenishing torrential rains, and when it does, its force against rock is incredible; three million tons a year are moved out of Zion and on to Lake Mead where it joins the Colorado. One of the Virgin's tributaries, Pine Creek, is a potent example of what has happened at Zion. When the Zion-Mt. Carmel Road was tunneled through Bridge Mountain, six windows were cut into the mountain face for view-points along the highway. The debris — tons of rock — was thrown into Pine Creek basin below. Within a few months, flash floods from summer rains roared through Pine Creek with mighty force and completely ground the rubble and carried it on downstream. The Virgin River "seethes like a thing alive, a serpent devouring red watery tons of mud and sand from countless tributaries," wrote a park ranger. "We stand awestruck as enormous boulders crash and split asunder. Uprooted cottonwoods tumble and upend like jackstraws."

Zion's architecture is Navajo sandstone: sand dunes built on a desert plain for millions of years, slowly cemented in layers, and then washed and crumbled away. The brilliantly colored monoliths left standing were named by the Mormons: Great White Throne, Angel's Landing, The Sentinel, Towers of the Virgin. Zion itself means "The Heavenly City of God." It is a land of "peace and comfort," as they said, but to the geological eye, this is a less than harmonious landscape. The thrones and towers and sentinels stand as mute testimony to millions of years of erosion typical of southern Utah and the Colorado Plateau.

Right *Zion's architecture is Navajo sandstone — sand dunes built on a desert plain for millions of years, cemented in layers, then washed away.*

Below *Named by the early Mormon settlers, the Three Patriarchs stand sentinel over Zion National Park.*

Left   *Looking south towards Angels Landing from the entrance to the Narrows in Zion National Park.*

Inset   *Water flowing on either side of Weeping Rock is transformed into a delicate curtain as the sun catches the rivulets of water.*

Below   *Composed of cross bedded Navajo sandstone, this dramatic colonnade in Zion National Park stands festooned with ponderosa pine.*

PETRIFIED FOREST NATIONAL PARK

The Southwest's grand terrain, with its canyons, deserts, craters, and abundant early American habitats, has over the years presented geologists and archeologists with a gold mine of exploration opportunities. Scientific theories about everything from what happened to the Anasazi to how many "shallow seas" once covered the land abound. As the sciences and their measuring instruments become more sophisticated, the theories sift out and pronouncements are made with more confidence. Still, there are vast mysteries for which no matter of analysis will resolve. One of the most prominent is dinosaurs. The paleontologists have now reopened the casebook, just within the past decade, and the final word is up for grabs.

Another mystery is the petrified trees along the Puerco River and the Painted Desert. There is general agreement now, but precisely what happened at this remote spot of northeastern Arizona still eludes science. There are some splendid guesses, and, although rock strata and their revelations of the land will not be denied, some more startling theories have been advanced.

Two hundred million years ago, Arizona, that is the Southwestern states, was a tropical land situated some 1700 miles closer to the equator than it is today. One must accept the relatively recent theory of plate tectonics to imagine shifting continents finally joined into the shapes we recognize, but whether a tropical landscape to the south, or just here, fossilized evidence points to some strange creatures and plants.

At one time, tourists took away fossil remains and chunks of petrified logs by the wagonload. Now these relics of 200 million years of geological history are protected in Petrified Forest National Park. The detail pictures show gem-like quartz crystals caught in silicified wood.

This high dry tableland was once a vast floodplain crossed by hundreds of streams and rivers. To the south, tall, stately pine-like trees grew along the headwaters. Crocodile-like reptiles, fish-eating amphibians of gigantic proportions, and small dinosaurs lived among a variety of ferns, cycads, and other plants and animals — all of them known only by their fossils. The tall trees — given names like Araucarioxylon, Woodworthia, and Schilderia — fell and were washed into the floodplain. There they were covered by layer after layer of sand and mud from distant mountains, and upon all that, great layers of volcanic ash. Water rich with silica from the ash seeped through to the trees and bit by bit replaced the original wood tissues with silica deposits. Slowly the silica hardened, and, without oxygen to expedite decay, the trees turned to stone.

That had to be in the late Triassic period, according to all calculations, for certainly the land was not done with its transformations. After all that, the Colorado Plateau went through its slow but violent upheavals, thrusting the now petrified trees and their ancient companion plants and animals to the surface where wind and water began the desert's erosion processes. Erosion continues to break down the giant logs found on the surface, and, interestingly enough, dig a little deeper for what geologists are convinced is more of the same, perhaps some 300 feet of fossil-bearing material yet to be seen. The National Park Service policy is to protect and preserve what we have, for this is perhaps the one park subject to the most vandalism through the years.

Cutting a living from this harsh land is difficult now, and, no doubt, was just as difficult 2000 years ago, when, as evidence shows, humans first lived here. We don't know the full story, but there were separate occupations, a cultural transition from wandering families to settled agricultural villages — pueblos — and trading ties with neighboring villages. Then this story of early people, told by potsherds, rubble and petroglyphs, fades about 1400 AD.

In the mid-1800s, U.S. Army mappers and surveyors came into the area and carried back East stories of the remarkable "Painted Desert and its trees turned to stone." Next came farmers, ranchers, and sightseers.

A German artist by the name of BALDWIN MÖLLHAUSEN may have been the one who triggered, quite innocently, the run on petrified wood as a souvenir. Accompanying a military expedition in 1858, MÖLLHAUSEN wrote:

> WE COLLECTED SMALL SPECIMENS OF ALL THESE VARIOUS KINDS OF FOSSIL TREES, AND REGRETTED THAT AS OUR MEANS OF TRANSPORT WERE SO SMALL WE HAD TO CONTENT OURSELVES WITH FRAGMENTS, WHICH CERTAINLY SHOWED THE VARIETY OF PETRIFICATION, BUT NOT THE DIMENSIONS OF THE BLOCKS....ALL THE WAY WE WENT WE SAW...GREAT HEAPS OF PETRIFICATIONS GLEAMING WITH SUCH SPLENDID COLORS THAT WE COULD NOT RESIST THE TEMPTATION TO ALIGHT REPEATEDLY AND BREAK OFF A PIECE, NOW OF CRIMSON, NOW OF GOLDEN YELLOW, AND THEN ANOTHER, GLORIOUS IN MANY RAINBOW DYES.

By the 1880s, when the railroads came through and brought tourists by the wagonloads, "the temptation to alight repeatedly and break off a piece" was too much. No one knows just how much of the petrified forest was lost in the next 20 or 30 years, but by the turn of the century it had become staggering. Logs were being dynamited for crystals to be used as commercial abrasives. Such exploitation threatened to simply wipe the whole place off the earth before how it got there in the beginning could be determined.

Fortunately, there came a respite in the abrasive market and in the gap Petrified Forest National Monument became a reality. In 1932 some 2500 acres more of the Painted Desert were purchased, and in 1962 was given national park status.

Above *Newspaper Rock in the Painted Desert, Arizona, is a fine example of Indian petroglyphs, a reminder that man has struggled to survive in this less than hospitable environment for many thousands of years.*

GRAND CANYON NATIONAL PARK

On a recent rainy day at the South Rim of the Grand Canyon, a car stopped and a man jumped out and walked to the rim. He called back, "Don't get out, Mildred. It's too cloudy. You can't see a thing." At that very moment a bolt of lightning streaked from the sky about three miles to the northeast. Quickly he shouted, "Grab the camera and turn off the motor, Mildred. I think we've got something here."

FRANCOIS E. MATTHES wrote in *The Grand Canyon of the Colorado River,*

"THOUGH THERE ARE ELSEWHERE DEEP CANYONS, SOME OF EVEN GREATER DEPTH THAN THE GRAND CANYON, . . . THERE IS NOT ONE THAT CAN MATCH ITS VASTNESS, ITS MAJESTY, ITS ORNATE SCULPTURE AND ITS WEALTH OF COLOR. WHOEVER STANDS UPON THE BRINK . . . BEHOLDS A SPECTACLE UNRIVALLED ON THIS EARTH."

Both men, eloquent in their own way, glimpsed in fleeting moments something for which the camera, the canvas, or the writer's words could not possibly have prepared them; a pageant of time so huge and complex, so foreign to the senses, and yet so

Below *An early winter sunrise highlights the low-lying clouds in the canyons and the snow on Hopi Point, Grand Canyon.*

incredibly beautiful, that it is at once a frightening reality and an illusion. The Grand Canyon is the climactic scene, the finale of the Colorado Plateau, the end of the course of the turbulent Colorado River before it flows on to the Gulf of California.

Search as one may for words — and you can stand along the South Rim and hear a hundred reactions in one day — nothing is adequate. It is better left unsaid, or, if nothing else, remember the words of a Texas cowboy who suddenly found himself near the edge while grazing cattle. He is reported to have exclaimed, "My God! Something happened here!" J. B. Priestley wrote: "Those who have not seen it will not believe any possible description. Those who have seen it know it cannot be described. . . . In fact, the Grand Canyon is a sort of landscape Day of Judgment. It is not a showplace, a beauty spot, but a revelation. The Colorado River made it; but you feel when you are there that God gave the Colorado River its instructions."

The Grand Canyon was first seen by white men in 1540, when a band of Coronado's conquistadors under Lopez de Cardenas came upon its south rim. For three days the Spaniards attempted to make their way to the river. Getting only one-third of the way down, they gave up and returned to the main party, and for the next three centuries the

Below   Caught at sunset from Desert View on the South Rim, Grand Canyon stretches forth in a "spectacle unrivalled on this earth".

Right *Waterfalls in their thousands have played a part in the creation of this unparalleled wonder.*

Below *Near Moran Point, another sunrise illuminates the banded sandstone walls and bathes the mountain peaks in fiery-red light.*

canyon remained a mystery and a legend. Then in 1857, an army lieutenant, Joseph Christmas Ives, reached the bottom. He wrote: "It seems intended by nature that the Colorado River, along the greater portion of its lonely and majestic way, shall be forever unvisited and undisturbed." It was left to a one-armed Civil War veteran, MAJOR JOHN WESLEY POWELL, a man of vision, to explore the Colorado and bring the wonders of the Grand Canyon to the world ... and to prove Lieutenant Ives wrong. His journals are fresh and vibrant and still used as guides along the river. And, astonishingly, his understanding of what happened here was remarkably accurate and has hardly been challenged. As he prepared to enter the Grand Canyon from the Little Colorado River,

Powell wrote: WE ARE NOW READY TO START OUR WAY DOWN THE GREAT UNKNOWN. WE ARE THREE QUARTERS OF A MILE IN THE DEPTHS OF THE EARTH, AND THE GREAT RIVER SHRINKS INTO INSIGNIFICANCE AS IT DASHES ITS ANGRY WAVES AGAINST THE WALLS AND CLIFFS THAT RISE TO THE WORLD ABOVE; THE WAVES ARE BUT PUNY RIPPLES, AND WE BUT PIGMIES, RUNNING UP AND DOWN THE SANDS OR LOST AMONG THE BOULDERS. WE HAVE AN UNKNOWN DISTANCE YET TO RUN, AN UNKNOWN RIVER TO EXPLORE. WHAT FALLS THERE ARE, WE KNOW NOT; WHAT ROCKS BESET THE CHANNEL, WE KNOW NOT; WHAT WALLS RISE OVER THE RIVER, WE KNOW NOT. AH WELL! WE MAY CONJECTURE MANY THINGS.

The last paragraphs of Major Powell's journal are perhaps the most eloquent of any descriptions. He was the first; he has not been surpassed:

THE GRAND CANYON OF THE COLORADO IS A CANYON COMPOSED OF MANY CANYONS. IT IS A COMPOSITE OF THOUSANDS, OF TENS OF THOUSANDS, OF GORGES. IN LIKE MANNER, EACH WALL OF THE CANYON IS A COMPOSITE STRUCTURE, A WALL COMPOSED OF MANY WALLS, BUT NEVER A REPETITION. EVERY ONE OF THESE ALMOST INNUMERABLE GORGES IS A WORLD OF BEAUTY IN ITSELF. IN THE GRAND CANYON THERE ARE THOUSANDS OF GORGES LIKE THAT BELOW NIAGARA FALLS, AND THERE ARE A THOUSAND YOSEMITES. YET ALL THESE CANYONS UNITE TO FORM ONE GRAND CANYON, THE MOST SUBLIME SPECTACLE ON THE EARTH. PLUCK UP MT WASHINGTON BY THE ROOTS TO THE LEVEL OF THE SEA AND DROP IT HEADFIRST INTO THE GRAND CANYON, AND THE DAM WILL NOT FORCE ITS WATERS OVER THE WALLS. PLUCK UP THE BLUE RIDGE AND HURL IT INTO THE GRAND CANYON, AND IT WILL NOT FILL IT. . . .

THE GLORIES AND THE BEAUTIES OF FORM, COLOR, AND SOUND UNITE IN THE GRAND CANYON — FORMS UNRIVALED EVEN BY THE MOUNTAINS, COLORS THAT VIE

Top   The Grand Canyon has been made by water; from its smallest ripple to the largest wave and rapid, the Colorado River scours and carves the canyon in some new way.

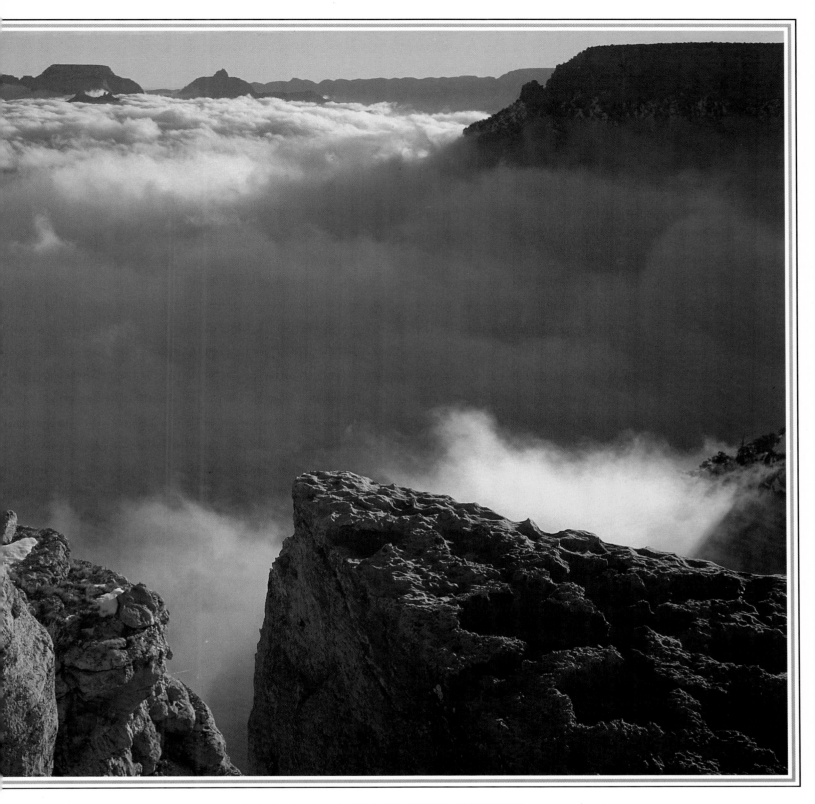

WITH SUNSETS, AND SOUNDS THAT SPAN THE DIAPASON FROM TEMPEST TO TINKLING RAINDROP, FROM CATARACT TO BUBBLING FOUNTAIN. BUT MORE: IT IS A VAST DISTRICT OF COUNTRY. WERE IT A VALLEY PLAIN IT WOULD MAKE A STATE. IT CAN BE SEEN ONLY IN PARTS FROM HOUR TO HOUR AND FROM DAY TO DAY AND FROM WEEK TO WEEK AND FROM MONTH TO MONTH. A YEAR SCARCELY SUFFICES TO SEE IT ALL. IT HAS INFINITE VARIETY, AND NO PART IS EVER DUPLICATED. ITS COLORS, THOUGH MANY AND COMPLEX AT ANY INSTANT, CHANGE WITH THE ASCENDING AND DECLINING SUN; LIGHTS AND SHADOWS APPEAR AND VANISH WITH THE PASSING CLOUDS, AND THE CHANGING SEASONS MARK THEIR PASSAGE IN CHANGING COLORS. YOU CANNOT SEE THE GRAND CANYON IN ONE VIEW, AS IF IT WERE A CHANGELESS SPECTACLE FROM WHICH A CURTAIN MIGHT BE LIFTED, BUT TO SEE IT YOU HAVE TO TOIL FROM MONTH TO MONTH THROUGH ITS LABYRINTHS. IT IS A REGION MORE DIFFICULT TO TRAVERSE THAN THE ALPS OR THE HIMALAYAS, BUT IF STRENGTH AND COURAGE ARE SUFFICIENT FOR THE TASK, BY A YEAR'S TOIL A CONCEPT OF SUBLIMITY CAN BE OBTAINED NEVER AGAIN TO BE EQUALED ON THE HITHER SIDE OF PARADISE.

Above *In a transient sea of fog, the Grand Canyon lays spread out in front of the South Rim, one of the most popular viewing sites.*

Facing page below *The Canyon in a different mood, still viewed from the South Rim.*

America's Wonderlands

IN THE WOODS, TOO, A MAN CASTS OFF HIS YEARS, AS THE SNAKE HIS SLOUGH,
AND AT WHAT PERIOD SOEVER OF LIFE, IS ALWAYS A CHILD.
IN THE WOODS IS PERPETUAL YOUTH. WITHIN THESE PLANTATIONS OF GOD,
A DECORUM AND SANCTITY REIGN, A PERENNIAL FESTIVAL IS DRESSED,
AND THE GUEST SEES NOT HOW HE SHOULD TIRE OF THEM IN A THOUSAND YEARS.
IN THE WOODS WE RETURN TO REASON AND FAITH.

RALPH WALDO EMERSON

On June 30, 1864, the United States Congress passed an act granting the Yosemite Valley to the State of California "upon the express conditions that the premises shall be held for public use, resort and recreation." Such a grant of land was without precedent, unknown in the affairs of governments the world over. Scenic and hunting preserves had been the prerogative of European royalty, but nowhere had land ever been set aside for all the people.

Once done, conservationists saw an opportunity to begin a system by which the federal government could set aside valuable wildernesses in the name of the people of the nation, *for the people of the nation.* On March 1, 1872, the first *national* park, Yellowstone, was established "as a public park or pleasuring-ground for the benefit and enjoyment"... *of all the people.* By 1890, three more sites had been made national parks, including Yosemite, now deeded back to the federal government from California.

The heritage bequeathed Americans by those who set aside Yosemite and Yellowstone has endured. And it has never been more eloquently expressed than in the legislative act establishing the NATIONAL PARK SERVICE:

TO CONSERVE THE SCENERY AND THE NATURAL AND HISTORIC OBJECTS AND THE WILDLIFE THEREIN AND TO PROVIDE FOR THE ENJOYMENT OF THE SAME IN SUCH MANNER AND BY SUCH MEANS AS WILL LEAVE THEM UNIMPAIRED FOR THE ENJOYMENT OF FUTURE GENERATIONS.

The variety of national parks is one of the joys of knowing about and visiting them. They range from the old, rolling, forested mountains of the east, to the snow- and glacier-covered peaks of the west, from the arid deserts of the Rio Grande, to the volcanoes of the Hawaiian Islands.

BIG BEND NATIONAL PARK

Previous page left *Underneath the lush growth of Hawaii Volcanoes National Park, the earth seethes and boils, sometimes releasing steam above the surface to further moisten the tropical environment.*

Previous page right *Beautiful but frightening, this 1961 Kilauea eruption at Halemaumau spread a river of boiling lava down the side of the mountain, engulfing everything in its path.*

Below *The Torrey yucca plant or Spanish dagger survives with almost no rainfall, in the harsh climate of Big Bend National Park, Texas. And despite its hostile nature, many animals and plants take full advantage of what the desert has to offer.*

Right *The Rio Grande defines the southern boundaries of the park for 107 miles. For thousands of years the river has carved its way through the Chisos Mountains and across the desert, creating an arcing linear oasis as it flows.*

Nestled in the arid, rugged, and forbidding great curve of the Rio Grande River in southwest Texas lies Big Bend National Park, where man meets the conflicting forces of nature; a land of incredible heat and freezing cold, virtually without rainfall, yet blooming with life, high mountains and deep basins, great distances and microscopic life, gentle beauty and desolate surroundings, brooding silences and the lilting song of a wren.

For one hundred miles along the southern boundary of Big Bend National Park — and the border between the United States and Mexico — the Rio Grande winds its way first southeast and then abruptly northeast, still carving, as it has for eons, through desert and mountain. This is the harsh country where Texas ranchers once called eighty thousand acres of pastureland over-stocked with two mules. Yet there is a singular beauty about this place.

The Indians said that after making the earth, the Great Spirit simply dumped all the leftover rocks on the Big Bend. Spanish explorers, less poetic and less intimate with the landscape, merely dubbed it "the uninhabited land." Would that it were that simple to explain or understand. The geology of the Big Bend country is complex. Like much of southwest Texas, it was under shallow seas millions of years ago. As the continent heaved this way and that, some of this land was exposed and great swamps grew, harboring dinosaurs and huge, winged reptiles. And then the continent shifted again, this time pushing up the Rockies and the Sierra Madres. Here the Chisos Mountains sprang up between the two. Thousands of years later, the Rio Grande began to carve its way through this mass of twisted rock. Now, at times, it seems to be the only living thing to have survived.

The name Big Bend refers to the great U-turn the Rio Grande makes here in Southwest Texas. The river is an arcing linear oasis, a ribbon of green strung across the

dry desert and cutting through its mountains. As do all rivers that survive desert passages, the Rio Grande has its headwaters outside this desert. It is the Rio Grande, that defines the park's southern boundary for 107 miles.

The great Chisos Mountains that thrust up 6000 feet above the arid floor of the plain — one peak is 7835 feet above sea level — are an unexpected oasis in the middle of the park. It is the southernmost mountain mass in the United States and one of the attractions for the increased visitation to Big Bend National Park. This is a bird-watchers' mecca. Over two hundred species have been seen here.

Despite its hostile nature, history has not passed Big Bend. Prehistoric Indians made their homes here at least ten thousand years ago. These people were not farmers, but hunters and gatherers, taking only what this country offered on its own.

More than 200 plant and animal foodstuffs were here for the taking, but the vastness of the desert necessitated that people be semi-nomadic to take advantage of them. Their diet included walnuts, persimmons, the fruit and blossoms of yucca, the fruit and young pods of pricklypear, and mesquite beans. They fashioned baskets and

Below *Cutting through the Chisos Mountains at Santa Elena Canyon, the Rio Grande River widens out to a passive flow.*

sandals from lechuguilla fiber and yucca leaves. For hunting they used the atlatl, a throwing stick that propelled stone-tipped darts to kill deer, rabbits, and other game. We know that some of Big Bend's desert springs have been flowing for thousands of years, because Archaic Culture sites are commonly concentrated around today's spring. These sites may include rock shelters and hearths, or fire rings.

By AD 800, another culture appeared that was more slanted toward hunting than gathering. By 1200, the La Junta Culture, a Puebloan people, dominated; they were desert farmers. In the 1500s, however, the Spaniards enslaved these people and substantially changed their culture. The Apaches and Comanches moved in sometime in the 1700s; both tribes used Big Bend as a stronghold and last bastion for survival against the white man. By the late nineteenth century the U.S. Army had firmly established command. With the exception of 1916, when there was a brief flourish of Mexican arms from across the border, the Big Bend country has been quiet.

Big Bend became a national park in 1944, with the help of the Texas Legislature, and it is one of our most magnificent preserves.

Left and below *Among the cacti grow* Lupinus harvardii *or Texas Bluebonnet, a splash of bright color against a dusty green background* Echinocereus chloranthus *cactus also blossoms in the desert with this colorful result.*

ROCKY MOUNTAIN NATIONAL PARK

The Rocky Mountains are a part of a much larger system of mountains in the Western Hemisphere, the cordillera (Spanish for "chain of mountains"), which runs 10 000 miles from Patagonia to Alaska and divides the Atlantic and Pacific drainage systems — the Continental Divide. The Southern, or Colorado, Rockies, the Middle Rockies in Wyoming, the Northern in Idaho and Montana, and the Canadian, make up the North American part of the chain. Rocky Mountain National Park preserves a 40-mile portion of the Continental Divide in the middle of the Southern portion, no less than 65 peaks rising above 10 000 feet, more than 400 square miles of virtually unspoiled nature and scenic splendor set aside by the federal government in 1915.

In nearly every park story — at least those that have great geological stories to tell — some reference is made to the formation of the Rocky Mountains, that upthrust and folding that took place some 300 million years ago. This is, indeed, a point of reference, for that upheaval of what we now believe to be plate tectonics had an effect on the entire western United States. About 150 million years ago the plastic mantle rock

Below *Running along a north/south axis, the Rocky Mountains are part of the cordillera which runs the length of the continent. For unspoiled nature and scenic splendor, Rocky Mountain National Park cannot be beaten.*

beneath the earth's crust formed a trough, or geosyncline, where the Rocky Mountains are now located. A sea filling this trough deposited layers and layers of sediment that later became rock strata. Then about 90 million years later this strata folded and uplifted to heights of 20 000 feet. Erosion wore the mountains down to hills; some 40 million years later the whole process started over. The last erosion process is still going on, the mountains we see being worn down to their granite core. Finally, about a million or so years ago, the Ice Age came — perhaps several of them — and sent great glaciers cutting and carving through the mountains and valleys. Men saw none of this, of course, but scientists do believe that several of Rocky Mountains' small glaciers may be the remains of the Ice Age — Andrews Glacier, along the Continental Divide, may be one, and it can be reached by several trails.

The human history of Rocky Mountain National Park goes back some 15 000 years ago when nomads crossed the Continental Divide hunting game. Indian tribes roamed the mountains in later years, so an occasional artifact reveals, but very little is known of their camps, if any, or their identities. Zebulon Pike, for whom Pike's Peak is named,

Below *Spanish Peaks at Big Sky in the Rockies — it is possible to see, even through the snow, the gradations of vegetation ranging from coniferous forests on the lower slopes to tundra on the peaks.*

came to the mountains in 1806; Colonel S.H. Long, who gave his name to the park's highest point, led a party to the foothills in 1820. It was not until 1860, however, that the first family settled in the mountains. Joel Estes built a cabin in what is now Estes Park; he stayed six years. But the one person who did the most to elevate these mountains to national park status was Enos Mills, who came here in 1884 at the age of 14. Around 1900, Mills began a campaign at his own expense to interest the authorities in creating a park. He lived to see the dedication on September 4, 1915. Ironically he died in 1922 as a result of a subway accident in New York City.

The snow-mantled peaks of Rocky Mountain National Park rise above green alpine valleys and glistening lakes. One third of the park is above tree line, and here tundra dominates — a major reason why these mountains and valleys have been set aside as a national park. Rocky Mountain is a unique park; every elevation change opens a different world, from the valley to the peaks. At lower levels, open stands of ponderosa pine and juniper grow on the slopes facing the sun; on cooler north slopes are Douglas fir. Gracing the streamsides are blue spruces intermixed with lodgepole pines. Here and there appear groves of aspen. Wildflowers dot meadows and glades. Above 9000 feet, forests of Englemann spruce and subalpine fir take over. Openings in these cool, dark forests produce wildflower gardens of rare beauty and luxuriance, where the blue Colorado columbine reigns. At the upper levels of this zone, the trees are twisted, grotesque, and hug the ground. Then the trees disappear and you are in alpine tundra — a harsh, fragile world. Here more than one-quarter of the plants can also be found in the Arctic. From valley to mountaintop, Rocky Mountain is truly of many worlds.

Rocky Mountain National Park preserves a 40-mile portion of the Continental Divide, where more than 65 peaks rise above 10 000 feet. But alpine meadows, glistening lakes and tall stands of pine and spruce make it a park of great diversity.

YELLOWSTONE NATIONAL PARK

Yellowstone is a wonderful and mysterious land which has intrigued the minds of men and moved them to great and inspired thoughts. The sheer wonder, the mystery, and the beauty of this high mountain plateau challenged the early explorers. Here in Yellowstone were features of such significance that men were inspired to evolve a new philosophy for the land; a new land-use ethic based on preserving a part of our natural scene for the future.

This is where the National Park System really began. There are those who will argue for Yosemite, but Yellowstone was the first National Park established by the U.S. Congress in 1872. To many, Yellowstone is a fleeting glimpse of a geyser or an elk or a canyon, but certainly it is more than this. Yellowstone is an idea, a philosophy, and a monument to farsighted conservationists who more than a century ago foresaw the need to preserve a bit of primitive America; a symbol of America's reverence for the foundations of her greatness, the great untouched North American wilderness.

In Yellowstone the two contrasting elements, fire and water, have combined to produce a land of natural wonders. It is a land born in the fires of thundering volcanoes and sculptured by glacial ice and running water into a fascinating landscape.

Although thousands of years have passed since Yellowstone's violent birth, the thermal features in the park bear testimony to the fact that, at a comparatively shallow depth beneath us, the fiery hearts of the volcanoes still beat. Literally thousands of hot springs dot the thermal basins; gigantic columns of boiling water are hurled hundreds of feet into the air causing the ground to shake; hissing stream vents punctuate the valley floors; and stumps of redwood forests buried by volcanic ash and petrified in an upright position stand out starkly on eroded mountainsides.

More recently, glaciers have reworked the land's surface by smoothing canyons and leaving a myriad of sparkling blue ponds and lakes scattered across the landscape. And now, mountain streams carve beautiful canyons and leap over resistant rock ledges in breathtaking cascades and waterfalls.

Geologically, Yellowstone is a young land, with the last of the lava flows burning their way across the surface less than 100 000 years ago. Soil development is shallow and pioneer plants are common. Even today fire and water, in the form of thermal heat,

Right *With the force of a raging giant, the lower Falls of the Yellowstone River thunders over the narrow lip of the precipice to the river basin below.*

Below *The first national park established by the U.S. Congress in 1872, Yellowstone embodies the ideals of farsighted conservationists who saw the need to preserve a bit of untouched North American wilderness.*

Above   *The Yellowstone River braids and spreads across the floor of Hayden Valley in Yellowstone National Park, flanked on either side by dense coniferous forests.*

Right   *In winter the bison come down from the high country to the valleys attracted by the warmth of the hot springs and the hope of a more plentiful supply of food*

Right above   *Yellowstone is a land born in the fires of volcanoes and sculpted by glacial ice and running water into a fascinating landscape. Minerva Terrace is one of these spectacular wonders.*

Far right   *Thousands of hot springs dot the thermal basins, boiling water is hurled hundreds of feet in the air by the pressure exerted beneath the surface of the earth. Old Faithful, the most famous of these geysers, attracts many thousands of visitors every year.*

snow, and rain, dominate the landscape and determine which plants and animals will make up Yellowstone's natural communities.

No one believed the stories from the early explorations of the Yellowstone country. "Thank you, but we do not print fiction," wrote the editor of *Lippincott's Magazine*. One reviewer of an article on Yellowstone wrote that the author "must be the champion liar of the Northwest." And so Yellowstone remained a mystery until 1870 when a military survey team issued their official report.

Lieutenant Gustavus Doane, a young cavalry officer on the Henry Washburn surveying expedition in 1870, climbed a mountain and tried to describe what he saw. "A single glance at the interior slopes of the ranges," he wrote, "shows that...the great basin has been formerly one vast crater of a now extinct volcano. The nature of the rocks, the steepness and outline of the interior walls, together with other peculiarities, render this conclusion a certainty." The public believed.

In one of those rare moments in history when everything seemed to fall into the right place, Doane's report came at a time when Henry David Thoreau and Ralph Waldo Emerson were writing essays on conservation. "Why should not we...have our national preserve," wrote Thoreau, "in which the bear and panther and even some of the hunter race may still exist and not be 'civilized off the face of the earth'...for inspiration and our true re-creation? Or should we, like villains, grub them all up for poaching on our own national domains?"

Washburn, whose expedition had consisted of some prominent people, led the march on Congress. Yellowstone, as yet untouched by those who would exploit the land, had to be saved, he said. The idea had been discussed in the wilderness. "It was at the first camp after leaving the Lower Geyser Basin," wrote Cornelius Hedges, a lawyer and correspondent, "when all were speculating which point in the region we had been through would become most notable, when I first suggested uniting all our efforts to get it made a national park, little dreaming such a thing possible."

It was the worst possible timing. The country, still reeling under the strains of the Civil War, economic instability, and the throes of westward expansion, faced the harsher realities of life. Words like *aesthetics, natural beauty,* and *inspiration,* were viewed with great suspicion. It was all quite natural. The unnatural thing was that such idealism ultimately prevailed. Yellowstone National Park was established in 1872.

Left *The Grand Canyon of Yellowstone National Park from Grand View. The erosive power of water is evident — mountain streams carve these beautiful canyons and leap over resistant rock ledges in breathtaking cascades and waterfalls.*

Above *The elements fire and water give rise to numerous oddities in the park. Stumps of redwood forests, petrified in an upright position stand in the Opalescent Pool at Black Sand Basin. The Grand Prismatic Spring (upper inset) and the Algae beds (lower inset) provide a startling contrast of colors.*

Grand Tetons National Park in Wyoming incorporates mountain peaks, alpine lakes and sagebrush flats within its scenic domain. This park is inhabited by moose, elk, trumpeter swans and other wildlife.

YOSEMITE NATIONAL PARK

When the first journalists found their way into Yosemite Valley in the 1850s and announced to the nation that America had treasures beyond compare, it was a cultural shock of extraordinary proportions. Thomas Jefferson had said that the view of the confluence of the Potomac and Shenandoah rivers at Harpers Ferry, Virginia, was worth a trip abroad; but the great westward expansion was hardly even a dream and writers like James Fenimore Cooper was saying that "as a whole it must be admitted that Europe offers to the senses sublimer views and certainly grander than are to be found within our borders." America was suffering from an identity crisis, but Yosemite changed all that. We had found our castles and great works of art in the granite spires and giant trees of certainly one of the most beautiful spots on earth.

"As I looked at the grandeur of the scene," wrote one of the discoverers of Yosemite Valley in 1851, "a peculiar exalted sensation seemed to fill my whole being, and I found my eyes in tears of emotion." The Valley is only one-half of one per cent of what would become the park, yet it is the park itself. It was first seen by the white man when two miners, tracking a wounded bear, entered the sacred ground of the Indian. "Uzumati," they called it. It was awesome. Cliffs so high and granite mountains so huge they staggered even the most hardened explorers; nearby giant Sequoia trees, so old they defied any known means of measuring time; waterfalls that came from the sky and plunged into eternity; and a wilderness so vast and remote that to this day man has not seen it all.

Below *America found her castles and great works of art in the granite spires and giant trees of Yosemite, surely one of the most beautiful spots on earth. Reflected in Tioga Lake these "granite spires" overwhelm the horizon.*

Right *Down through the heart of the Sierra Nevada Mountains, a stream cuts through to the valleys below.*

We know Yosemite best through the camera and the poet. Ansel Adams remains the master photographer, but it was JOHN MUIR, the naturalist, who influenced generations of conservationists and led the national park movement throughout the country. Muir went into Yosemite in 1868, and in mind and spirit never came out. He was obsessed with the mountains and wrote eloquently:

I DID NOT GO TO THEM FOR A SATURDAY, OR A SUNDAY, OR A STINGY WEEK, BUT WITH UNMEASURED TIME, AND INDEPENDENT OF COMPANIONS OR SCIENTIFIC ASSOCIATIONS. AS I CLIMBED OUT OF YOSEMITE TO BEGIN MY GLORIOUS TOIL, I GLOATED OVER THE NUMBERLESS STREAMS I WOULD HAVE TO FOLLOW TO THEIR HIDDEN SOURCES IN WILD, UNTRODDEN CANYONS, OVER THE UNNUMBERED AND NAMELESS MOUNTAINS I WOULD HAVE TO CLIMB AND ACCOUNT FOR — OVER THE GLACIAL RIVERS WHOSE HISTORY I WOULD HAVE TO TRACE, IN HIEROGLYPHICS OF SCULPTURED ROCKS, FORESTS, LAKES, AND MEADOWS…WHERE NIGHT FOUND ME, THERE I CAMPED. WHEN I DISCOVERED A NEW PLANT, I SAT DOWN BESIDE IT FOR A MINUTE OR A DAY, TO MAKE ITS ACQUAINTANCE."

Below *Shot from an unusual angle, Half Dome or the great Tissiak rises to a height of nearly a mile.*

Right *Named after the three sons of Chief Tenaya captured by the Mariposa Battalion, the Three Brothers stand along the north wall of Yosemite Valley.*

Far right *Bridal Veil Falls sends a gauzy spray over a wide area, creating rainbows and damping the leaves of big-leaf maple growing at the foot of the Falls.*

The nation had not witnessed such devotion to nature. He gave us Yosemite, and with it he set the future for all environmental and conservation movements.

ONE IS CONSTANTLY REMINDED OF THE INFINITE LAVISHNESS AND FERTILITY OF NATURE — INEXHAUSTIBLE ABUNDANCE AMID WHAT SEEMS ENORMOUS WASTE. AND YET WHEN WE LOOK INTO ANY OF HER OPERATIONS THAT LIE WITHIN REACH OF OUR MINDS, WE LEARN THAT NO PARTICLE OF HER MATERIAL IS WASTED OR WORN OUT. IT IS ETERNALLY FLOWING FROM USE TO USE, FROM BEAUTY TO HIGH BEAUTY.

To simply say that Yosemite Valley is beautiful beyond description is to rely on Adams and Muir. It must be experienced. El Capitan, the largest single block of granite on the earth, is poetry in itself. Its moods, like the walls of the Grand Canyon, change with the hour, the day, the season. See it in the morning sun, or with slight traces of snow clinging to tiny ledges on its nearly sheer face, and you have found an image indelible for life. El Capitan's massiveness, and that of Half Dome, Glacier Point, and other mammoth peaks and pinnacles, is at first frightening; should they come crashing down in some cataclysmic earthquake, it would seem the world would end.

Left *El Capitan is the largest single block of granite on the earth. Its colors and moods change with the hour, and with the season.*

Below *Scaling El Capitan's "Delectable Pinnacle", this climber is shown against the backdrop of Yosemite Valley and Cathedral Rocks.*

Far left *Sierra redwoods edge Mariposa Grove, in Yosemite National Park. One of these giants is the amazingly grotesque Grizzly Giant. It is possible to drive a car straight through the base of some of these redwoods.*

Yosemite Valley is a mosaic of open meadows sprinkled with wildflowers and flowering shrubs, oak woodlands, and mixed-conifer forests of ponderosa pine, incense-cedar and Douglas fir. Wildlife from monarch butterflies to mule deer and black bears flourishes in these communities. Around the valley's perimeter, waterfalls, which reach their maximum flow in May and June, crash to the floor. Yosemite, Bridal Veil, Vernal, Nevada, and Illilouette are the most prominent; some of these have little or no water from mid-August through early fall.

Glaciers, mighty rivers of ice hundreds of feet thick, created Yosemite Valley and cut away the face of Half Dome; the winds and rains rounded and polished, and today they continue their work. But these same glaciers and the same winds and rains have given us more than what we see here. Yosemite Valley is only a fraction of what Muir experienced and wanted set aside for the public: Tuolumne Meadows at 8600 feet; Mount Lyell, 13 114 feet, on the eastern crest of the Sierra; and giant stands of the Sequoias, one tree measuring 209 feet tall and 34 feet in diameter. Muir saw it all: "the most songful streams in the world...the noblest forests...the loftiest granite domes...the deepest ice-sculptured canyons." In seven continental life-zones Yosemite captures the most exquisite wildflower and delicately laced moss, the fiercest and most rugged of mountains, where nothing grows and only the stout-hearted little marmot scampers across the rocks, and then frames it all with roaring, icy streams and incredible silences. "These sacred mountain temples are the holiest ground that the heart of man has consecrated," Muir wrote, "and it behooves us all faithfully to do our part in seeing that our wild mountain parks are passed on unspoiled to those who come after us, for they are national properties to which every man has a right."

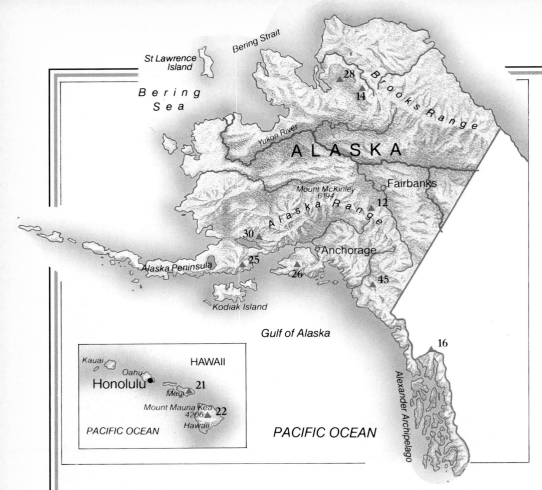

NATIONAL PARKS OF AMERICA

1 ACADIA NATIONAL PARK, PO Box 177, Bar Harbor, ME 04609

2 ARCHES NATIONAL PARK, 446 S. Main St, Moab, UT 84532

3 BADLANDS NATIONAL PARK, PO Box 6, Interior, SD 57750

4 BIG BEND NATIONAL PARK, Big Bend National Park, TX 79834

5 BISCAYNE NATIONAL PARK, PO Box 1369, Homestead, FL 33030

6 BRYCE CANYON NATIONAL PARK, Bryce Canyon, UT 84717

7 CANYONLANDS NATIONAL PARK, 446 S. Main St, Moab, UT 84532

8 CAPITOL REEF NATIONAL PARK, Torrey, UT 84775

9 CARLSBAD CAVERNS NATIONAL PARK, 3225 National Parks Hwy, Carlsbad, NM 88220

10 CHANNEL ISLANDS NATIONAL PARK, 1901 Spinnaker Dr., Ventura, CA 93001

11 CRATER LAKE NATIONAL PARK, PO Box 7, Crater Lake, OR 97604

12 DENALI NATIONAL PARK AND PRESERVE, PO Box 9, Denali, AK 99755

13 EVERGLADES NATIONAL PARK, PO Box 279, Homestead, FL 33030

14 GATES OF THE ARCTIC NATIONAL PARK AND PRESERVE, PO Box 74680, Fairbanks, AK 99707

15 GLACIER NATIONAL PARK, West Glacier, MT 59936

16 GLACIER BAY NATIONAL PARK AND PRESERVE, Gustavus, AK 99826

17 GRAND CANYON NATIONAL PARK, PO Box 129, Grand Canyon, AZ 86023

18 GRAND TETON NATIONAL PARK, PO Drawer 170, Moose, WY 83012

19 GREAT SMOKY MOUNTAINS NATIONAL PARK, Gatlinburg, TN 37738

20 GUADALUPE MOUNTAINS NATIONAL PARK, 3225 National Parks Hwy, Carlsbad, NM 88220

21 HALEAKALA NATIONAL PARK, PO Box 369, Makawao, Maui, HI 96768

22 HAWAII VOLCANOES NATIONAL PARK, Hawaii National Park, HI 96718

23 HOT SPRINGS NATIONAL PARK, PO Box 1860, Hot Springs National Park, AR 71901

24 ISLE ROYALE NATIONAL PARK, 87 N. Ripley St, Houghton, MI 49931

25 KATMAI NATIONAL PARK AND PRESERVE, PO Box 7, King Salmon, AK 99613

26 KENAI FJORDS NATIONAL PARK, PO Box 1727, Seward, AK 99664

27 KINGS CANYON NATIONAL PARK, Three Rivers, CA 93271

28 KOBUK VALLEY NATIONAL PARK, PO Box 287, Kotzebue, AK 99752

29 LASSEN VOLCANIC NATIONAL PARK, Mineral, CA 96063

30 LAKE CLARK NATIONAL PARK AND PRESERVE, 701 C St, PO Box 61, Anchorage, AK 99513

31 MAMMOTH CAVE NATIONAL PARK, Mammoth Cave, KY 42259

32 MESA VERDE NATIONAL PARK, Mesa Verde National Park, CO 81330

33 MOUNT RAINIER NATIONAL PARK, Tahoma Woods, Star Route, Ashford, WA 98304

34 NORTH CASCADES NATIONAL PARK, 800 State St, Sedro Woolley, WA 98284

35 OLYMPIC NATIONAL PARK, 600 E. Park Ave, Port Angeles, WA 98362

36 PETRIFIED FOREST NATIONAL PARK, PO Box 217, Petrified Forest, AZ 86028

37 REDWOOD NATIONAL PARK, 1111 2nd St, Crescent City, CA 95531

38 ROCKY MOUNTAIN NATIONAL PARK, Estes Park, CO 80517

39 SEQUOIA NATIONAL PARK, Three Rivers, CA 93271

40 SHENANDOAH NATIONAL PARK, Luray, VA 22835

41 THEODORE ROOSEVELT NATIONAL PARK, PO Box 7, Medora, ND 58645

42 VIRGIN ISLANDS NATIONAL PARK, PO Box 7789, St Thomas, VI 00801

43 VOYAGEURS NATIONAL PARK, PO Box 50, International Falls, MN 56649

44 WIND CAVE NATIONAL PARK, Hot Springs, SD 57747

NATIONAL SEASHORE AND MONUMENTS MENTIONED IN THIS BOOK

ASSATEAGUE ISLAND NATIONAL SEASHORE, Rt 2, Box 294, Berlin, MD 21782

CABRILLO NATIONAL MONUMENT, PO Box 6670, San Diego, CA 92106

CAPE COD NATIONAL SEASHORE, South Wellfleet, MA 02663

CAPE HATTERAS NATIONAL SEASHORE, Rt 1, Box 675, Manteo, NC 27954

FIRE ISLAND NATIONAL SEASHORE, 120 Laurel St, Patchogue, NY 11772

GULF ISLANDS NATIONAL SEASHORE (Florida Unit), PO Box 100, Gulf Breeze, FL 32561

GULF ISLANDS NATIONAL SEASHORE (Mississippi Unit), 3500 Park Rd, Ocean Springs, MS 39564

PADRE ISLAND NATIONAL SEASHORE, 9405 S. Padre Island Dr., Corpus Christi, TX 78418

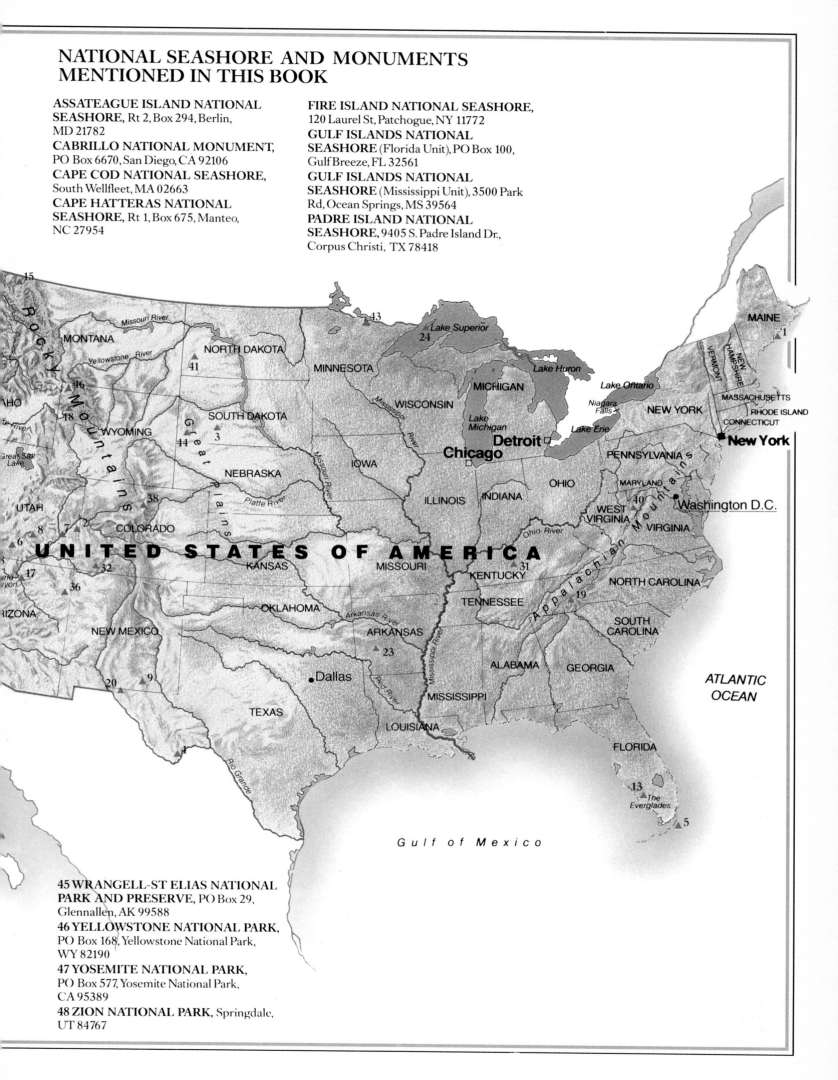

45 WRANGELL-ST ELIAS NATIONAL PARK AND PRESERVE, PO Box 29, Glennallen, AK 99588

46 YELLOWSTONE NATIONAL PARK, PO Box 168, Yellowstone National Park, WY 82190

47 YOSEMITE NATIONAL PARK, PO Box 577, Yosemite National Park, CA 95389

48 ZION NATIONAL PARK, Springdale, UT 84767

INDEX

PICTURE CREDITS

Ardea 22-23, 34, 35 bottom left, 56, 61 top, 82-83 bottom, 88, 90-91, 91 right, **Art Directors** 90 bottom left, 93 top left, **Biofotos** 24 inset, 36, 58 inset, 59 bottom right, 60, 72, 75 bottom right, **Camerapix Hutchison** 24-25, 52, 54-55, 82 top, 83 top, 84, 85 bottom inset, **J. Allan Cash** 29 top, 35 middle right, **John Cleare** 37 inset, **Bruce Coleman Ltd,** 20, 22 inset, 27 bottom, 32 top left, 37, 38 top, 48-49, 75 left, 77 right, 85 top, 85 top inset, **Stephanie Colasanti** 4-5 contents, **Colorific/Wheeler** 10, 12 inset, 28-29, 43 top, **Geoscience Features** 19, 70-71, **Image Bank** 1, ½ title, 6, 8-9, 11 top, 11 bottom, 12 left, 12-13 bottom, 14 inset, 14-15, 15 top, 16-17, 17 inset, 18, 19 inset, 32-33, 39, 40, 44-45, 46, 49 inset, 58-59, 64, 65, 66-67, 68-69, 70 bottom left, 74, 78, 79 inset, 81, 92, 92 bottom left, **Frank Lane** 35 bottom right, **Mountain Camera** 93 middle right, **Natural History Photographic Agency** 32 bottom left, 41, 43 right, 61 bottom, 62-63, **National Park Service** 31, **Oxford Scientific Films** 38 bottom, 73, **Photographer's Library** 2, 6-7, 42-43, 67 right, 68 top left, 89, 92 bottom right, 83 bottom, **Seaphot** 26-27, 27 top, 29 centre right, 29 bottom right, 83 bottom, **Spectrum** 53, 63 right, 68 bottom left, **Frank Spooner** 21, **Tony Stone Associates** 47, 57, **Vautier de Nanxe** 51 right, 80, 86-87, **Vision International** 30, 50-51, 76-77, 79,

Front cover: **ZEFA**
Back cover: **Art Directors**

Multimedia Publications (UK) Limited have endeavored to observe the legal requirements with regard to the suppliers of photographic material.